Your feedback and comments are always welcome.
Please feel free to contact us at:
thelittlehockeyhandbook@gmail.com

To Angelina and Liam

I hope you find the inspiration to reach all of your dreams. Thank you for helping me with one of mine.

TO THE PARENTS

A big thank you to all the hockey parents out there! All the early mornings, late nights and hours you volunteer at the rink are what makes the hockey world go round.

This little book is my effort to remind kids about some of the best parts of hockey and how we can all contribute to making this great game fun for everyone. With themes like Fair Play, respect and sportsmanship I hope to reinforce what is taught by coaches and federations around the hockey world.

I hope you and your children enjoy this book and have a great hockey season!

Coach Davidson

Hockey is Fun!

No matter which level of hockey you play in, the main goal is to have fun. Most professional players will tell you that when they were your age they may have been dreaming about playing in the professional leagues, but they were also having fun while working hard to achieve their goals.

Being involved in hockey gives you the chance to develop great friendships and lifelong skills and values like teamwork and respect. It also is a lot of fun! Kids around the world play hockey because it is a really fun and challenging sport. You have the opportunity to learn, compete and work together with some great kids in your community and from around the world!

Equipment

Your Stick: make sure that your sticks are the correct height for you (about up to your nose without skates on). This will ensure that you are in a good hockey position and not bent over and unbalanced.

Helmet and face guard: make sure that your helmet is done up correctly. Wearing a loose helmet can lead to injuries.

Body padding: leg, elbow, shoulder pad, jockstrap, hockey pants and gloves all should be in good condition and have a proper fit to ensure the most safety possible.

Uniforms: make sure that your jersey and socks are the correct size. Oversized uniforms make it hard to skate!

Skates: take care of your skates and protect the blades by using blade guards. Make sure that you have your skates sharpened regularly.

Goalies: you guys and girls have a lot of special equipment, but the guidelines are the same. Make sure your equipment fits you properly and that you maintain it all in good condition.

It is important that you look after your equipment. Each player has the responsibility to take care of his or her personal equipment. That means:

1. Making sure your equipment is clean (take home your stinky socks!!!)

2. Making sure that your equipment is all packed in your hockey bag after practice.

3. Making sure that you tell a parent or coach if a part of your equipment is broken, damaged or missing.

4. Making sure you have all of your required equipment for all practices and games.

Respect

Hockey is such a great sport, and to keep it great we need to respect those around us.

- ✓ Teammates – hockey is for everyone. No matter what a persons' background, ethnicity, gender or ability we should always show our teammates our respect.

- ✓ Coaches – your coach is helping you enjoy the great game of hockey. He or she deserves your respect and attention at all times.

- ✓ Opponents – without a team to play against there would be no hockey. Your opponents, just like your teammates, should always be treated with respect.

- ✓ Referees – refs are the third team on the ice that make hockey games possible. Even if you don't agree with a call, showing respect to the officials is a must.

- ✓ Parents and volunteers – without all the long hours your parents and volunteers spend behind the scenes organized hockey would not be possible. Hockey is built by hockey-moms and hockey-dads so show proper respect and appreciation for all that they do.

- ✓ Your club or team – be proud of your club and its heritage. Your uniform represents your club and you are an ambassador for your club, so be respectful of your clubs history and its future.

Fair Play

Fair play means that you should play hockey the way it is meant to be played, safe and fun for everyone.

By respecting your opponent, hockey can be fast paced, intense and safe for everyone. Hockey is a physical game and contact is an exciting part of the game. The rules of hockey allow for this exiting element while at the same time making sure that the players are as safe as possible.

When competing for loose pucks or finishing your checks, do so with proper technique. This allows you to play at a competitive level while ensuring all participants are safe on the ice. Ask your coach about your federations Fair Play guidelines and pay attention when he or she is teaching you about new skills like checking. Sportsmanship is also a part of Fair Play and it reflects on how we respect all those who are part of the game.

PENALTY BOX

In the locker room

Here are a few simple rules for how to behave in the locker room:

1. No horseplay. There is a lot of equipment in the locker room and no room for wrestling around.

2. Keep your sticks in the stick racks or by the door so that people are not tripping over loose sticks scattered all over the locker room.

3. Do not wear your skates around the locker room until you are ready to head out onto the ice.

4. Have control and be responsible for your own equipment.

5. Make sure your equipment is clean. Nobody likes to sit next to somebody with seven pairs of old socks in their hockey bag!

6. Keep the locker room tidy. If you wouldn't throw used tape on your moms' living room floor, then you shouldn't do it in the locker room either.

7. Don't be a mooch! Bring your own stick and sock tape.

At Practice

Most of the hockey season is spent at practice and this is where you and your friends get the chance to have a lot of fun, build your skills and compete against each other.

Practice time is most valuable when you give 100% effort. Remember that you get out of practice what you put in. This means that you will learn and have the most fun when you work hard and are dedicated to learning what your coach is teaching.

Here are 3 tips for having a great practice:

1. Always ask your coach questions if you don't understand a particular drill. Coaches are there to help you understand the game and to answer your questions.

2. Show respect for your coach and teammates by being on time and listening when the coach is talking.

3. Encourage and support your teammates.

Game time!

Finally! It's your chance to put all your hard work at practice to the test and play a game! Playing in games and tournaments gives you the chance to challenge yourself, work together with your teammates and have a lot of fun.

Here are a few things to keep in mind on game day:

1. Listen to your coach and what they have to say.
2. Work together as a team and support each other.
3. Be a good teammate and be positive to those around you.
4. Keep your shifts short so you have energy for the entire game.
5. Work hard and give 100% effort on every shift.
6. Play at both ends of the ice, be a two-way player.
7. Follow the Fair Play guidelines.
8. Be gracious in victory and defeat.
9. Drink lots of water throughout the game.
10. Have some fun out there! That's what hockey is all about.

Winning and Loosing

All teams in hockey will have their ups and down. That is part of sport, and that's what makes it exiting. When your team is on a hot streak enjoy it, but remember in order for you to win somebody else has to loose, so don't rub it in.

Hockey teams and players are a classy bunch and that means that there is no need for hot-dogging after a goal. It looks silly and it's not good sportsmanship. Celebrate with your line-mates, give high fives to your teammates on the bench and then get ready for the next face-off.

It is also important to support teammates and be positive. If somebody makes a mistake it is time for you to be a good teammate and be positive. Tell that player that it's ok or that we can do better next time. Hockey is a team game and that means we share the good and the bad outcomes as a team.

Off Ice

Even the biggest rink-rat can't be on the ice 24 hours a day, so here are a few tips for the off season or down times between practices:

1. Practice at home. All professional hockey players played pond hockey, road hockey or shot tennis balls in the basement when they were your age. Work on your skills with your buddies at home.

2. Cross train. Playing other sports helps you develop as an athlete. Other sports use different skills and muscle groups that can help you to be a better hockey player.

3. Watch hockey. Watch a game at the local rink or on TV. Having a favorite player that you can look up to is a great way to learn more about the game.

4. Get involved in your club. Volunteer to help with your clubs activities, try taking a referee course or volunteer as a water boy for your local team.

Setting Goals

Setting goals is a great way to motivate and inspire yourself to be the best hockey player you can be. By tracking your progress in specific skills you can see how you are progressing throughout the year.

When you set goals for yourself it is important to be specific. When you are specific about your goals it is easier to know when you have actually reached them. If, for example, you want to be a faster skater then your goal could be "I want to be able to finish a skating circuit in less than 45 seconds". This is something you can measure and test.

On the next page is a sample of a goal setting worksheet. You can make your own and add in any type of goal you want to work towards. Remember that you also need to say HOW you will accomplish that goal.

Goals	How will you test this goal?	How will you accomplish this goal?
Be a faster skater	Being able to finish the skating circuit in less than 45 seconds.	Focusing on my balance and power skating technique and by using 5 minutes before practice to work on this skill.
Win more face-offs	Winning at least 6 out of 10 face-offs on a consistent basis.	Spend 20 minutes per week with my Dad at home working on the 3 types of face-off draws.

You can make charts to help you follow your goals. Remember that there is a lot about hockey that you can't track in charts like having fun and being a good teammate. Often these are the most important parts of hockey, so keep in mind that these charts are only a way to help you follow your goals. Hockey is so much more than statistics.

On the next page is a simple chart that you can use. You can make your own charts and keep track of any type of skill. Just draw your own charts and add in any skills you want. You can rate yourself at the beginning of the year, at the midpoint of the season and again at the end of the year. This will allow you to see where you have progressed and where you need to work harder.

Name: _____	Start of Season	Mid Season	End of Season
Speed Skating Forward	★★	★★★	★★★★
Cross Overs Forward			
Skating Backwards			
Cross Overs Backward			
Quick Stop & Starts			
Wrist Shot			
Slap Shot			
Faceoffs			
Saucer pass			
Backhand pass			
Stretch pass			
Stickhandling			
Puck Control With Feet			
Penalty Shot Skills			
Communication			

DID YOU KNOW...

Hockey is played around the world! In Sweden it is called ishockey. In Finland it is called jääkiekko. In Russia it is called хоккей с шайбой and in the Czech Republic it is called hokej.

Even when the score isn't going your way you can still have fun and be positive. Hockey history is full of awesome comebacks, so keep working hard with your teammates and good things can happen.

Chances are pretty good that your team has a lot of interesting old stories and players in its past. Ask your team president about your clubs history, it's sure to be entertaining!

Colouring fun!

We hope you have enjoyed this book and that you have learnt a few things. We wish you all the best in your season and hope that it is full of great friends, fun practices, amazing games and fond memories.

Have some fun out there!